Contents

Annotation

By now the world population is more than 7.5 billion people.

And have you ever thought about how many of the people are happy? Are you happy? Are your relatives, friends, colleagues, and acquaintances happy?

There is the 21st century, but the number of unhappy people is increasing every day. In antiquity, people lived only to 35-40 years. Moreover, the living conditions of the early man were very dangerous; he was surrounded by wildness, predatory animals and birds, who willingly took the last food from him. Therefore, the life of an early man was not easy, and more likely it was not life, but it was survival. Early people lived in caves, which were the only haven. And what is now? In our modern world there is the Internet, advances in medicine, high-speed cars, comfortable apartments, entertainment to suit any taste, every year you can go on holiday to any part of the world, and nevertheless, many people are still unhappy.

So what's the problem?

First of all, we need to understand why people are unhappy, to find the root of the problem.

And this book is devoted exactly to this root of the problem. Here you will learn why many people of the 21st century are unhappy, how to deal with it and how to become happier.

Introduction

In this book, I want to share with you common to all mankind principles of interaction of people, which have already helped many people to become happier and it's most likely help you too.

First, we will give careful consideration of why there are so many unfortunate people today and why they are suffering. We will study the differences in the perception of happiness between boys and girls, the causes of a generation gap, the causes of ineffective teamwork, and how education affects all of this.

But things can't be all that bad as it may seem at first glance, because in our world there are enough opportunities to fulfill yourself, build a good house, grow a blossomed tree and bring up wonderful children. But the truth of the matter is that you should look from a different perspective.

It should be mentioned that in this book, there are both Russian and American examples, nevertheless, all examples are based on general principles from which you can derive benefit for yourself.

What do we know about unhappy people?

There are many of them, and every day it's still growing. They constantly use phrases such as "I am not happy", "I have a problem here", "I don't know what to do", "my life is a kind of empty and doesn't make any sense", "I don't understand where I'm going and why I live", "I can't achieve anything". And for most of these people, it seems that everyone around lives normally, and exactly those, who say like that, they can't cope with difficulties, because they don't understand how this life is organized.

On the one hand, I would like to calm a little bit such people, because they are not the only one such abnormal, but on the other hand, it seems like a distressing scene. And in general, the vast majority of people are unhappy, and moreover, this is a very big achievement to become a happy person.

Yes, this is not good, it seems to us, but why is this? Although not even "it seems", but definitely it's not good!

Why do people suffer?

Go down in history. If anteriorly people lived in wild conditions, many people lived in slavery, and those who lived in a free tribe, then they had some kind of war, and anyway, at any moment some Roman legionaries could come, chop you into pieces and make you live in another way. And now, it seems, what a paradise! You go to the sea, and you can go on a tour around the world, besides, there is an enormous LCD TV on the wall, which nobody even dreamed of 20 years ago, and nevertheless the many are unhappy. How comes it?

Well, here the reasons lie in a completely wrong upbringing and education. And I'm not a supporter of conspiracies, unlike someone I don't think that "this" is done systematically, purposefully, deliberately, maliciously, by some kind of world government, which have been conspiring to keep people unhappy because it's easier to manage them.

In different parts of the world, there are people, who are more or less happy, and there is normal management here and there. So what's happening?

Of course, all begins with the fact that this process is natural. Since it isn't a world government, it happens in itself. Why? Because we were brought up by our parents, and nobody trained parents in schools and universities how to bring up and what the outcome will be, there was nothing like that. Why did they not teach, how so? And what is about the state? Well, the state is something like a legal entity, this is a kind of idea. Well, in fact, it is created by people, and there is a natural origin, and everything that you have ever seen, for example, some houses, paper, pens, transport, hamburgers and all are created by people. To tell the truth, about the hamburger, at first there was nature, but then it was all transformed many times, and as a result, it was created by people. And here states, everything that we know about the state - all are invented by people, then produced, also all the rules are made by people. And the state doesn't know how to think in itself, which means that people should invent everything, do everything with their own hands.

And in order for something like that appears, parents are taught, we need to have a special person who will invent like this. For example, someone like Lenin, who thought a lot of things, wrote many texts, books, and as a result made other people their life better.

So we still need such people, but unfortunately, such people haven't appeared yet, those who would have risen through the ranks to the government and embed something, that they could tell to parents how to bring up properly. But now, it comes out that everything is letting it run its course - children grow up randomly, and besides, there is a direct dependence on material wealth.

What's happening to upbringing? About 200 years ago, there were serfs, their life was very complicated. It was necessary to work from morning to evening in order to feed somehow, in order to spend the winter at least somehow and not die of hunger, but also it was necessary to go to the landlord to work out – fulfill corvee, and only then you can sow and plow up something your part. And say yes, that in such conditions it's very difficult to cope with it because everyone must work. And just in order to work together, and everything went well, people had to cooperate.

And when satiety comes, when people have iPhones, when they can go on holiday every year, as a result, there is an effect, when food is always in abundance, and food will always be. Some people complain that they have a small salary, but at the same time, they will still eat. And it turns out that a person can choose with whom to communicate, and whom he can just ignore. And if someone is disgusting to him, if communication with someone doesn't go well, he will easily defend himself. For example, one student will just sit in his dorm on his bed and eat some hamburger and that's all. There is food and he lives, there will be a day - there will be food, there will be something new interesting, everything is fine, so he can just ignore other people.

When you read Russian literature over the past centuries, it's quite clear that there is whatever father in a family, for example, in a peasant family, he can be a veritable tyrant, but you have to use mechanisms to communicate with him. And so, people in our modern well-fed world have a unique situation: "I can ignore anyone, even my mother and father, but I will still be given food". And this situation leads to a very interesting socio-psychological effect.

It turns out that a person practically up to 30-35 years old, if he doesn't live in an independent marriage, which is completely separated from his parents, he practically doesn't know how life works, because some kind of office work with regular coffee, a smoking room and some kind of intrigues, gossips – it does not particularly teach how to live correctly. And even when a person there is more or less an expert at doing something, more or less cope with difficulties, he receives a stable salary, he goes on holiday, but it still doesn't teach how to live.

Take, for example, an army, where you need to live in a barracks, where there is an enclosed collective, and you can't come and go whenever you want, and you have to interact with these people every day, and this teaches how to live very well.

What do I mean by "teach how to live"?

But it is precisely the fact that when a person is allowed everything when a person can behave as he wants, and he is still given food, he doesn't know how effectively communicate with other people.

Life is arranged in a definite way. Imagine that life is a labyrinth where you need to cleverly walkthrough, and in some places, the walls are just smooth and firm, sometimes even soft, and somewhere they are very dangerous and with some kind of spikes that are also smeared with poison. And you walk in complete darkness through this labyrinth, and to live your life effectively, so that you navigate normally and you feel like a duck to water, so that you are on the rise and everything goes well in this life, so it's necessary to grope walls carefully, study this labyrinth and walk a lot, already knowing all by touch.

And you remember everything, make some kind of map, and it seems that darkness is around, but you, for example, outline everything on some tablet and can easily find it by touch. And then you go out and know where and how many steps to the left, to the right, and everything is going well, you are oriented in life, you know that half a step to the left, and here there are the dangerous spikes, and only half a step away from these and you can walk perfectly, and everything will be all right, because you will not touch any spikes. But you still need to walk carefully, don't stagger, so as not to hit, otherwise, it will hurt.

And instead, I mean, instead of learning all this and knowing that you grow up and from your childhood, parents give you money, but not to everyone, and you excuse me, please, if I hurt someone's feelings, of course, everyone live differently, and I condole with you, guys, if your life isn't sweet, but anyway, now most people have 'rich childhood' that there is always food in any case. And even if you quarrel with someone or something doesn't suit you, or you can't do something, or can't buy a phone such as you want, but there is still no threat of hunger, anyway. You can eat, and everything is fine, you live and breathe.

And then it turns out that you try different things, try different norms of behavior, and you escape all punishment, you are still given food, and it comes that you have an idea of the world as some big round hall with soft walls, that you can run here in the darkness wherever you want, you can rush straight to these walls, they are very soft, so you will be all right.

And then you find yourself, for example, as I said, in a marriage, where you moved somewhere else to another city, and your parents, they didn't have a good job, they just brought up you barely, and now you are working and you have to rent an apartment or you are mortgaged, where you live with your wife. And then it turns out that she was brought up doing what she wanted, and she escaped all punishment, and you were brought up doing everything you want. And it turns out that she wants to do things, which are convenient and pleasant only for her, and you want to do things, which are convenient and pleasant for you. And, of course, she starts to resent, because someone may claim some rights and say something that objects to her view somehow.

And what's more, there is such a terrible effect

Boys are very interested in girls, so girls from their youth are in such a state that boys are always around them, and they are ready to shut up, ready to endure any offense in order to at least be in the same room with her, only, oh, if you are together, even if she doesn't agree on sex, then at least walk by her hand, like saying I have a girlfriend, as you see, I am hook up with her, and everyone will say: "Wow, shocker! I can't do that, and you've got so close to her, wow!" And for young people it's so important that they just make any concessions, they tolerate everything. And it turns out that these girls, they live in full confidence that their life is real life. Moreover, if a girl really knows how to look after herself and she is able to behave decently at least a little bit, then she can easily attract men much older, and men will patronize and be profuse in compliments, and constantly offer any help to her, and so on.

And as a result, these girls just have a reinforced concrete view that life is like that, that they can really escape all punishment, do what they want. And one more funny thing is that you can't blame them for this, because, guys, seriously, put yourself in their's shoes, because you are the people who allow them to do it. And when later such a girl meets someone, but he already distinguishes who is this girl for real, because he has a great experience, because over the years he has learned the behavior of people. So he looks at a girl and he can see that after 20 years she won't be needed him for anything. That means she cannot be a good wife, she is absolutely a bad mother for his children, and if she tries to bring up children, she will fail, it will be just awful, therefore this guy can't have children with her, he will never want this. For him, it will be generally the bottom action on Earth - to have children with such a girl.

Well, and she lives for consumption, i.e. her interests are completely different, not like he has, and she will still suck out money from him if he contacts her, and in general, even abed, she can't bring him any pleasure. And he looks at her, but his 'function' is turned off, that in order to be in the same room with her, he will tremble and tolerate everything. And he has another view: if you want to be pleasant to him, then be pleasant, behave yourself, respect his interests, for example, be sweet and charming. If you just chat, like a just pretty girl, then he won't be interested. If you say at least one word wrongly at him, or you just somehow unpleasantly express yourself, he will object to you or make a remark. But at the same time for a girl, it's usually such a shock: "What is it all about?", "I didn't even break anything, but you make some observation, who do you think you are?"

And again, this is a situation in which you can't blame the girl for this. Also, this guy has a perfect understanding of her mind, why she sees in this way. And it comes out, in the life of such a girl this guy is an indicator of how life works.

Here is one more example. At first, a girl is such a bimbo, and then, when she is a wife, and when she is ugly, awkwardly lying on the couch, she cannot get up, because she is on the eight months pregnant, and her husband comes home from work, he is tired, but besides sex, before he didn't get anything from her, and now he cannot get even a sex, and instead of understanding of her defenseless situation, she used to do what she wants all the time and communicate as she wants, she also yells at the husband, calling him bad names. Although she isn't value for him, there is no interest and benefit to him, but she continues to scold him.

And naturally, the husband loses control of himself: "Who do you think you are?" And he immediately begins to tell her "who she is" and "who her mother is", that's where life really works, i.e. the girl is in a vulnerable position, and now she doesn't represent any value, her husband communicates with her simply on common to all mankind principles.

Yes, we talk a lot only about girls, and of course, we will mention guys too. But in general, for girls, as a rule, it's a shock to encounter with someone who communicates with them on common to all mankind principles. Where you need to deserve friendliness, where everyone doesn't tiptoe by you, but where you need to deserve everything. Where you say something pleasant – somebody smiles at you, you don't say something pleasant - people look at you neutrally, say something careless – people eye you askance, if you say something sharply – they frown, when you say something sharply two times – you be turned out of the door. And for girls, it's a shock.

But what about guys?

As to young guys, of course, it's not so prevalent, because, on the contrary for many guys, it's necessary to run after the girls, to adapt to them, to be very kind and nice.

Of course, not many people cope with this, but on average guys are always strung up. They still need to achieve a girl, they need to say something special in order to take her fancy. That means guys have this basic idea, that what you need is to say such a way to like your girl.

But unfortunately, it works only with sexual drive. Communicating with each other, guys absolutely ignore this, but not exactly they ignore these rules, but rather simply they don't think about their existence.

Also, when I walk down the street, I constantly observe what is happening around me, where people absolutely don't know how real life works, and absolutely don't know how to contact well, interact with other people.

For example, a very widespread situation, when young people go somewhere either occupying the whole sidewalk, or some company goes on my side of a large sidewalk, and there are so many of them, so I can go only around them and it's very far, but they only need to move a little, and they don't do this. Or at least last people need to move back, but they also don't do this. And when I walk along my side, on the very edge, and I have no place to go, and when we are getting closer, as a rule, young people literally take a short step to the side, so they come together with me in half a body.

And it turns out that they don't want to move on, and I have nowhere to go. And they just bump into me and scuff half of my body by half of their body, and just pass on, and they are absolutely fine, they don't feel any discomfort.

How comes it? They just go by their company, they push each other, touch each other, and when strangers meet them, then scuffing a stranger is absolutely normal for them.

Many people simply have no idea that it's possible for some person to be unpleasant. You see, there are no representations?

How education has an impact on happiness

And now, I want to come down to the second factor, which greatly influences on this picture. As I said at the very beginning there is no special bringing up. People are just fed. And yes, you can do what you want, and we still love you, we still give you food. And the second factor is the education system when people are gathered into isolated groups, parity of years, placed in their special room, where they sit, run and interact almost exclusively with each other. They don't communicate effectively with people of different age and they don't mix with teachers, they communicate with them only about the school subject.

And the children go together from one study room to other room and interact only with each other, and it turns out like Justas Walker is talking about, who is a cheerful milkman on YouTube, a very wise well-read man, an American, who lives in Siberia. He said that at homeschooling, when children study at home and then pass tests at school, it turns out, that they get used to interacting with people of different ages. At home, they need to communicate with everyone, with elder brothers, sisters, with younger brothers, sisters, if you have younger neighbors, younger, older children, because all grow differently. Then they have to communicate with dad, mom, grandfather, grandmother, and neighbors, and they are of a different age too.

And then the child comprehends the rules of communication with different generations. And he understands everything, he has an idea of how relevant this is, there are older people, and he fully understands everything about them, he sees that this is an integral part of our life. And in the same room, there can be an older person and a child who is younger than him, and other family members should simultaneously interact normally with both the older person and the child, and then a system of communication is developed for this.

But a person who is sent to school, so he comes there, he communicates from morning to evening only with his coevals and then he comes home. He has a lot of thoughts and emotions about whom he has met, who has hit him, who has beaten somebody, and who is needed to revenge, who has a very cool phone, where his class wants to go, to which event. And he has all thoughts somewhere there, at school.

And he talks to parents "Bye-bye". His cup of emotions is emptied because of school, yes, he pours in all his life energy there, and then he comes home, and he doesn't need anything, he needs to relax, just plays PlayStation, and we immediately get the standard "mom, dad, leave me alone". That mean the parents for him automatically become "ancestors".

And that's all, it comes out, that a new generation, it gets this opportunity to develop completely in isolation. They go to school for many years, and there some processes which influence on them, they have some kind of new fashion, some new ideas about the world, other styles of communication, and they get used to living in such a way, and the children continue to lose communication with their parents. And as a result, when there are some close interactions, it turns out, that for years it wasn't just strangers, but they become estranged more and more from each other, and it happens gradually. It can take many years and the result is parents don't understand children at all, and children don't understand parents at all.

You see, there is education system, it encourages this situation when people eat and eat all the time, and they can behave as they want, and they are also in isolated conditions so that any new trends can come, take root, and during this time communication with parents could be lost.

Work in a team

And so, these people, when later they get married, they are indoors with each other, and they hate each other, because they have a sharply conflicting value system, and they face a task that they don't even know how to solve, because logic is also not taught in schools, no one has a high-quality mechanism, and therefore, when such a problem arises, that one person wants everything to be as he wants, and the second person wants everything to be as he wants . And how do they find some middle ground, how do these gears work together, of course, they don't know, because there is no analytical mechanism, and they don't understand how to come to some kind of decision. And how to be in this situation, because it's just awful!

But again, this is an example of marriage, but I hope you understand, nevertheless there is still a need to work together, by some kind of team. A trivial example, when you open your own company, and there should be a team, and the more this company develops, there should already be a decent number of chiefs, and other employees.

But people are used to living only for their interests, every employee who comes is interested in stealing, every boss is interested in screwing all subordinates over, and moreover, he despises all of them, he only wants to catch hold of money, he "remembers" other workers hundred times. And how to be? After all, an effective system fails.

For example, the deceased Steve Jobs, once he told in his interviews that he started with a company that located in a garage and there were few people, and after 10 years he had four thousand employees and 10 billion dollars - and this is the coolest startup in the world, and he also said that for him the staff, the human resource, was very important, he always chose the best one, he worked with the best, that is why he was so cool. And he said, when he needed to say goodbye to someone, he would say goodbye, although it was very hard, he did it anyway. And only by the best team there was created something very, very good, and now they are ahead of the curve in this industry. And Steve was right!

So, how to create a team of the best, if all the participants don't understand at all how to communicate with each other? There is a good example, there are a husband and a wife, at some point they begin to hate and despise each other, but colleagues, some bosses, business partners, who are co-owners of a business, exactly the same way each of them hogs a blanket: "Look here, who are you?", "And then who are you?"

Or there are people united by the fact that they served in the army together or they went to the same school somewhere, for example, they sat at the same desk for many years: "Okay, okay, I know you", "And I know you". And then, when 'it' is coming, it turns out that everyone wants more money, so that everything is for one, and the second person is nothing, and here it turns out that for the first time we will know, that there are suchlike problems. Why? Because before they escaped punishment because they always were fed.

Attempts to help

And you see, it's not clear how to massively get rid of this. Therefore, we must try to convey these ideas to people.

But as already mentioned, when there is a person too spoiled, because there simply material wealth played a role, the person lived all the time, and he had the opportunity to ignore anyone, if he doesn't like them - he can block them, and that's all, he just continues to sit eating a hamburger.

And when someone appears and shows that such behavior is unacceptable, and tells him how life does work, then this person is perceived as a crank. And a girl or a guy, who used to communicate with some weird friends, again who they won't like, this person will be blocked on Facebook or Instagram or somewhere else, but who will go to their favorite party, of course, they will communicate and walk with them.

And now, when such a person faces me, he concludes in the same way that apparently only I'm a real monster here, and other people are normal, as they always are, and he doesn't need to listen to me.

And, it comes out, that all these people, they are absolutely not adapted to do something effectively together, like a team, they can't do this at all.

Leaping ahead, human happiness depends largely on relationships with other people, i.e. who is very good at building up relationship with people around, who has many friends, happy relationship with relatives, he is happy, friendly and smiles a lot, but who doesn't get this, who is constantly unsociable and dissatisfied, of course, those are unhappy and their things are all wrong.

I recently bought a salad in a supermarket, and when there are few of these salads, they are divided into packages and sold at a discount of 50 percent, and at that moment the woman was doubtful whether to take it or not to take. It was evident that it was for the first time. Then I came up and said: "Don't doubt, I took this many times, and I had only 1 of 30-40 a little bit spoiled, and I didn't eat this, so everything is normal here, everything is always good, moreover in two times cheaper. " Also I said to believe my eyes because they say true.

And she was such a not very beautiful woman, it was evident that she was keen on junk food, she had greasy skin, moreover, there was her daughter the same pear-shaped, ugly and unhealthy. And she looked at me in such a way and said: "I don't want to trust anyone, much less to a man." And she said that with such sarcasm, although I was absolutely friendly, even with care idea. And she gave it out in such a voice "especially a man".

And such people, they live lonely, unhappy, unhealthy, do you understand? So that woman isn't satisfied with her life, because she doesn't go fleeting gait along the street with thoughts: "Yes, I've just got nasty with a young man, yes, and I'm happy". Not at all, these people are unhappy, and they still live in such a way. And it's not clear how to convey to them, where life is real, how to convince this idea to them, that the way you behave is all temporary because then you will encounter situations, where you still need to interact with other people.

One more example: I am going down the stairs, and a woman goes with a baby carriage, and she needs to go it down an uncomfortable staircase.

There is a baby in a carriage, and it's very difficult to go downstairs by herself. Of course, I come up and say: "Shall I help you?". So I used casual, friendly voice, like a matter of course. But she says: "Mm, oh, no."

And I was so surprised. So she hesitated, as if she hadn't expected and said this "no", that it sounded sharply and confidently. Well, for me, freedom is a sacred relic, I don't force people, I don't impose myself. I told to her: "As you say." And I left. I told her that "as you say" without any hints, without anything, it was absolutely normal "as you say."

But it was obvious that her child was absolutely small in a carriage, i.e. she became a mother quite recently, so before the baby, about two years ago she was still a bimbo, and that's all. And now, apparently, nobody offers to help her at the entrance yet, and on the street, she didn't have to lift the baby carriage. Passersby didn't offer any help, and it's clear that the woman isn't ready to interact with people. But take my word for this, when several years later you will find this woman, and you will meet her with her second child, and again she won't understand how to descend the carriage by herself, and you will offer to help her, and she will say: "Yes, yes, of course, thank you very much!" Because over the months, over the years, an understanding will come to her that otherwise, she can't cope. And it will be necessary to learn how to ask for help, and she will gradually learn this. And again, even having learned this, she won't learn everything else, i.e. to learn something you need to have a certain situation.

And you see, the trouble is that a person is only confronted with the need to build effective communications, and do some co-operative work productively and be happy, smile to each other, and only after, when nothing works, conflicts come up, when you are punished already for this, when it becomes very painful, offensive, there are some great losses, only then the learning process begins. And over the months, over the years, a person will learn, at least a little bit of something, but as to other aspects, there is nothing as before.

And of course, purposeful upbringing from a young age, with the help of adequate explanations, like how something works, that's the point that would save a child. A child would grow and not be like girls who "I take everything that I want due to my beauty", but at the same time they are absolutely not able to give pleasure to their man, and for example, if you want to educate properly you can use the books of the Dale Carnegie or someone else experienced in relationship. You can refer to any sources on how to effectively interact with people, for example, how a very good seller knows how to communicate with clients, then such a girl, of course, she will keep every Tom, Dick, and Harry at arms' length, then she will choose a man, whom she likes, who is really good, which gives joy and pleasure. And she will behave properly, i.e. on universal common to all mankind principles, she will give pleasure to him, and at the same time she will be valuable, attractive, and then a man will be deliriously happy, and a woman's self-rating will also grow very much. Because "Look how I give pleasure to him and how he is happy, and it is so complete feeling, look, how this man is happy with me." And he won't leave anywhere, he will want to be only with her.

You see, such global transformations occur when people know how to communicate on universal common to all mankind principles.

You know, it took me so many years to learn to not automatically see some girls like sexual objects. When a girl can come to me and I talk to her only in a formal way, and we talk about something useful, and I don't have any bad thoughts, because this is just communication, when I know that I need this person for some work, but of course, sometimes there might be another situation, I can have some romantic feelings, and then I communicate differently.

And yes, I have learned this mechanism, and I communicate with people on common to all mankind principles. And like I said many people are just shocking by me: "Why are your ideas so terrible." And I try to explain that this is a preparation for real life, but unfortunately, people can't recognize this.

So there is something like this argument. And as I said before, it's not clear how to massively change it quickly, but I'm absolutely sure, that some of you are more enlightened than others people are, and you will hear my message, and you will understand that you see a little bit another side of your life, that this round labyrinth with very soft walls is not all. And you will start asking me about this labyrinth, and you yourself will start to see, and you will recognize and feel that somewhere you have been hurt unfairly, and you will think how it's, maybe, and it is exactly what the author told me.

After all, if you are pleasant infinitely to some man, he wouldn't be short with you, so you start to think, that you don't know how to please some man? How is that? And what could he need from you?

So if you are a man, and he is a man, then you doubt that he wants you like a sexual object, although this can also be, but less often, but even more, if it's not the reason, then again emerges the question as to what he wants from you, maybe there is something about a job? Well, if in the case he wants nothing from you, then he doesn't need you at all. And in the light of the fact that you don't need him at all too, you try to communicate with him as it's convenient for you, but he can get angry at you, so it happens that in a real life like this, where nobody owes anything to anyone, it's your style communication doesn't work? And you ask: "Wow, what can I read about this, and how should it work, how can I communicate effectively on common to all mankind principles?"

In general, guys, I'm sure that there are such people among you, who will be interested, and you will definitely make progress, and you will become much more pleasant, and what is the most important, you become effective and successful people, because a person, who understands these principles and knows how to communicate, he gets a key to a new life, where all is better for him.

You will be screwed nowhere, this is especially true for guys, but for girls, it's very important too, but at the same time they have a big catch until a girl has a grain of beauty, there will always be a man who wants her.

Fatal girls' error

And it turns out, that the fatal mistake of girls is that if someone wants to obtain a girl, she thinks, that she is already perfect, beautiful, and she doesn't need to develop anymore. And this is a huge mistake. With the passing of years, it becomes clear, that different men always want her, but she is still unhappy, because they only wanted to shack up with her, or somehow else use her for their own purposes, but they don't give happiness to her, because they are not the men, because strong and confident, intelligent, developed, advanced men pass by her, they don't like her, they don't ask for her phone number, they pass by, she doesn't know how to give pleasure them. And those people, who want her, they are just some inadequate, with inferiority complexes, who simply don't have enough sex in life, and therefore they run after the girls. And then a girl makes a false conclusion.

And you know, she bears children to one man, then to another man, she loses her green, her beauty, and somewhere under forty she starts to give much thoughts, that maybe she did something wrong in her life, although "it's bullshit, it can't be true, probably it was just a feeling". But I hope that some of the girls will also think about this.

The main explanation of why people are unhappy

And now let's talk about the most important example, which will fully help you understand, why people in the modern world are still unhappy.

Lucy is a representative of generation Y, the people born in the late 70s - early 90s. Now they are 25-40 years old, they have graduated from universities and are working now. If they work in a big city and are engaged in intellectual work, they are called "Yuppie" - young urban professionals, young employed citizens. Lucy is like that. In general, Lucy is fine. So why is she so unhappy?

Let's clarify where happiness comes in the most basic sense of the definition. Surprisingly, the formula is simple:

"The level of happiness = reality - expectations."

Nothing tricky. If you expect more than you get — you are unhappy. If, conversely — you are happy.

It's interesting, that objective reality plays a secondary role. It doesn't make a person happy or unhappy in himself, so it does only in combination with expectations. If the child is expecting Xbox for his birthday, and he will get a simple bike, he is likely to be upset. If he is expecting at least some bike, and he will get the best sports model, he would flip out.

So, it's clear about happiness: to be happy, your reality should exceed your expectations. So why does our Lucy have inflated expectations? To better understand this, let's get to know her parents.

Lucy's grandparents are representatives of the "great generation." They grew up approximately during the Great Depression when The US economic crisis in the 1930s was. In early youth, they observed poverty and unemployment. During World War II, they also served or worked in a factory, where they could meet.

After the crisis of the 30s and the military 40s, the prosperous 50s came: the real sector is growing, everyone has a job, there is enough money. War veterans (then they were twenty years old) are given preferential mortgages, American architects began typical cottage development in the suburbs, young families got an affordable house, cars, TVs and other items of the American dream.

Grandparents marry (in large quantities, that means in the whole generation), and they had children. There was a population explosion namely "baby boom". America was filled with happy children of the 50s, who would see poverty only in documental films.

Grandfather and grandmother teach their children that the most important thing in life is stable work and steady income. They want their children food to be delicious and the grass in the yard green. And now their children, Lucy's parents, have grown up with thoughts about a stable and longeval career.

Lucy's parents know, that they will definitely get this green. They just need to work a lot.

As for the career expectations of parents, they successfully went through the hippie culture in the 70s and then joyfully set about their careers. And there in the 80s and 90s, the American world is experiencing unprecedented economic growth. Everything grew into all fields of work, money is everywhere, it only needs to earn.

Our heroes are brave and confident people. They honestly worked and earned even more than they planned. And they bought a better house, and life was more comfortable. So to maturity, they formed a general feeling of life satisfaction.

And it turns out, that Lucy's parents didn't see the war before and a protracted economic crisis. They are sure that everything will always be good and you just need to work. And they brought up their Lucy with the same idea, but in even they do this in a more extreme way as if her possibilities are endless, and Lucy, and all her peers, can become anyone they want.

The 90s was coming. On television there are the young "Backstreet Boys" and live Cobain, and the little boys and girls sipped the idea that they were unique, their possibilities were endless, and the whole world had a green light for them. Moreover, the sad fate of parents who simply achieved financial stability doesn't suit them. Stability is boring. In the life of generation Y, amazing things must happen. Flowers will surely bloom on their yard.

Then there is the first fact about Lucy. She is extremely ambitious: "I can, of course, become the president of the United States. But is this my calling? Do I really want to become a politician? No, that would be a compromise for me ... "

Lucy and her peers don't want just a comfortable life and prosperity. It isn't enough for them. If Lucy's parents achieved the "American Dream", then Lucy will achieve her own, unique, dream.

I should make a caveat, that Lucy and her peers want the material wealth not less than their parents do. But at the same time, they want the work to bring them satisfaction. "Baby boomers" even didn't think about this.

However, Lucy isn't only extremely ambitious. From early childhood, her parents inspired her: "You are special!"

And now it is high time to talk about the second feature of Lucy and her friends. They live in a fantasy world. "Of course, we all will achieve happiness and success in life. And we all find an amazing job and we make money with satisfaction. But I am special, I am. So, my life will also be special,

I will leave a mark in history and will stand out in a crowd", Lucy thinks in college classes. And now we have a whole generation of Lucy, who is not only convinced that flowers will bloom on their yards, but each Lucy is convinced that as soon as she finishes university, her yard will become especially beautiful, and a magic unicorn pony will soar above this.

This delusion is going to play a cruel joke with Lucy when she obtains a diploma.

If Lucy's parents were preparing for years for hard work, then Lucy is confident that she is so special and wonderful, will be given the job easily. She just needs to choose the direction she likes and waits until her talent is discovered. This is how Lucy sees her career in high school.

But, alas, real work is blood, sweat, and tears, even if you don't aim at a colorful green with unicorns. To build a non-outstanding, but at least a sustainable career, it will take you many years of outstanding work. For such a life Lucy didn't prepare. She expected another that she would become the new Jobs-Zuckerberg.

But she won't, her wishes and dreams are not enough. But she isn't ready to accept it.

Professor Paul Harvey is a known expert of Lucy and psychologist, explored the worldviews of people of the Y generation. He notes, that his representatives "have unrealistic expectations from life and an unreasonably high opinion of themselves," and also "painfully resist criticism". "Without putting enough efforts, nevertheless such people continue to expect a great reward from life and continue to be disappointed ", writes Harvey.

Despite the fact that Lucy has the highest opinion of herself, our reality has another opinion. And that's where our Lucy is two years after high school. Our heroine has built unrealistic expectations from her work, and naturally, was disappointed. Because of the discrepancy between expectations and reality, she is unhappy.

But that's not all. There is another problem that exacerbates Lucy's position. Everything seems to be mocked at her. It is clear, that among the generation of Lucy's parents, someone is richer and someone is happier. But since most of the parents didn't use Facebook and Instagram, they are not particularly aware of how their peers' career has developed. They just lived and minded their own business. And at best they look around only the neighbor's green.

But Lucy is pursued a new-fashioned social phenomenon, there is hooey on Instagram. Because of social networks, Lucy lives in a world in which a) people constantly publish information about themselves; b) what they publish is often not true; c) in general, others share their successes and keep quiet about their failures.

If you look at a Facebook page or Instagram of a typical classmate of Lucy, then there will be only parties, meeting famous people, trips abroad, gifts from fans and expensive restaurants. And nowhere it is written that she actually earns money at a club as tequila girl, borrows money from her parents, and bought these roses herself. This is called "image making".

And because of this Lucy has the feeling that everything is fine around everyone, but she was the only one, who got nowhere, she has achieved nothing in life. That's why Lucy looks small. And although she is likely to begin her career successfully, she suffers from a sense that she is a loser.

Not all is lost! Let's review the results

But I will make your day because not all is lost! What I would advise to such as Lucy, so to remain as you are ambitious. In the world there are enough opportunities to be realized, you just need to set and do. Maybe everything will turn out wrong as you planned, but something will definitely work. The main thing is to keep to work hard. Stop to consider that you are very special. The truth of life is that you are an inexperienced young man, who so far has nothing to offer the world. In order for this, you need to work hard, really hard. Do keep your character. Now nothing is worth to make an image of a wealthy and successful person. If your friends and acquaintances seem successful, don't rush to conclude. Perhaps they just hold the iPhone the right way. You need to do your job, then there will be no reason to envy others.

In general, guys, all this is a matrix, this is full life, it has hidden the truth from you, you don't have the opportunity to see how life really works, how communication really works, and therefore constantly it turns out that someone doesn't want you, someone doesn't love you, someone doesn't wait for you, and this is terrible, and I want to help you with these problems.

And this is just the beginning, I will write many useful explanations, that can help you.

I hope it was interesting, see you soon.